영어로
설교하기

주상현 지음

영어로 설교하기

발 행 | 2024년 05월 27일
저 자 | 주상현
펴낸이 | 한건희
펴낸곳 | 주식회사 부크크
출판사등록 | 2014.07.15(제2014-16호)
주 소 | 서울특별시 금천구 가산디지털1로 119 SK트윈타워 A동 305호
전 화 | 1670-8316
이메일 | info@bookk.co.kr

ISBN | 979-11-410-8661-9

서문

영어가 제2외국어인데 영어로 복음을 전하거나 설교할 수 있나요? 나이가 많은 나이에 미국에 오셨다면 한국어와 완전히 다른 영어발음을 완벽하게 구사하는 것이 쉽지 않습니다. 그럼에도 불구하고 영어로 설교할 수 있나요? 소수민족 교회에서 자기 모국어로 설교하는 것이 대부분인데 어떻게 영어로 설교를 할 수 있을까요? 대답은 '예'이며 제 경험을 잠시 나누도록 하겠습니다.

저는 만 25살에 미국에 왔을 때 영어발음이라는 진짜 도전에 직면했습니다. 미국에 오기 전 한국에서 여느 중고등학생처럼 영어를 공부했고 문법과 읽고 쓰는 것은 어느정도 했지만 미국에서 실제로 영어로 말하기와 듣기에 있어서는 여전히 많은 어려움이 있었습니다. 미국 도착한지 한 달 후, 저는 미국 사람들의 말을 듣고 이해하는 데 약간 익숙해진 느낌이었습니다. 하지만 영어로 말을 걸 때는 여전히 어려움을 겪었는데, 많은 사람들이 제가 영어로 말하는 내용을 이해하지 못했기 때문입니다. 그래서 무엇이 문제인지 곰곰이 생각해봤어요. 문제는 문장의 문법이나 구조가 아니라 제 발음이었습니다. 저는 제가 적절하게 말하고 있다고 믿었고 저와 같은 1세 한인들은 제 영어를 알아들었지만 정작 영어 원어민들은 제 발음을 알아듣지 못했습니다. 이 점이 저에게 큰 도전이 되었고 저는 하루 속히 영어 발음을 개선하는 데 집중하기로 결심했습니다.

저는 텍사스에서 온 미국 학생에게 영어 발음 도움을 요청했습니다. 하지만 우리 둘 다 어디부터 시작해야 할지 어떻게 해야 할지 알지 못했습니다. 저는 발음을 빨리 향상시킬 수 있는 가장 좋은 방법이 무엇일까 고민해 보았습니다. 그리고 영어 사전을 찾아보니 영어에는 44개의 발음 기호가 있다는 것을 알았어요. 그래서 저는 이 44개의 발음만 정복하면 되겠다는 생각을 하게 되었고 거기서부터 시작하기로 결정했습니다. 친구에게 44개의 소리와 몇 개의 단어를 예로 들어 각각 발음해 달라고 부탁했어요. 전체 세트를 녹음하는 데 10분이 걸렸어요. 하지만 이것은 저에게 획기적인 전환점이 되었습니다. 매일 몇 시간씩 그가 녹음해 준 소리를 연습했죠. 일주일이 지나고 2주 후, 저는 일부 영어 모음이 생각보다 어렵다는 것을 깨달았습니다. 저는 이전에 제 영어 모음 발음이 괜찮다고 믿었는데, 이제 그 발음이 모두 틀렸다는 것을 깨달았죠. 그래서 장모음과 단모음을 모두 연습하는 데 많은 시간을 할애했습니다. 그 후 자음 발음 연습으로 넘어갔어요. 약 3개월이 지나자 돌파구가 보이기 시작했습니다. 영어 단어 발음이 크게 향상되었어요.

원어민들과 대화할 때도 제 말을 훨씬 더 잘 알아듣기 시작했어요. 하지만 거기서 멈추지 않았어요. 집에서는 발음할 때 제 입 위치가

올바른지 확인하기 위해 항상 거울 앞에서 연습했습니다. 또한 제 발음을 정확하게 듣기 위해 손바닥으로 제 귀를 반쯤 가리고 연습했습니다. 또한 제 목소리를 녹음해서 원어민의 목소리와 비교하기도 했습니다. 운전할 때는 길거리나 건물에서 보이는 단어는 무엇이든 발음해 보았습니다. 6개월 동안 이렇게 했더니 영어 발음이 크게 향상되었습니다. 향상되었는 줄 어떻게 알았나요? 제가 한인 교회 중고등부 목사가 되어 처음으로 영어로 설교를 시작했기 때문입니다. 놀랍게도 사람들이 저를 어린 나이에 미국에 온 1.5세 인줄 알았다면서 영어 발음을 칭찬했습니다. 발음을 개선하기 위한 노력이 결실을 맺은 것 같아 매우 감사했습니다. 6개월의 집중적인 연습이 필요했지만 그 결과는 상당했습니다.

이 책에서는 제 영어 발음 개선 방법을 공유하여 여러분도 스스로 연습하면서 영어 발음이 향상되는 경험을 할 수 있도록 돕고자 합니다. 제가 이 책을 쓴 것은 제 실력 향상을 자랑하기 위해서가 아니라, 복음을 전하는 사역이 한 언어에 국한되지 않고 다른 언어로도 확장될 수 있도록 간단한 발음 개선 방법을 나누기 위해서입니다. 하나님께서 제 삶에서 일하시기 시작한 것은 한인 교회에서의 사역뿐만 아니라 미국 내 다른 민족에게 복음을 전할 수 있는 문을 열어주셨기 때문입니다. 영어는 이들 그룹이 서로 소통하는 언어이기 때문입니다. 저는 세계 각지에서 온 여러 유학생들에게 매주 영어로 성경을 가르치며 사역을 했습니다. 이를 통해 난민과 이민자들에게 사역할 수 있는 문이 열렸습니다. 하나님께서는 제가 미국의 다양한 민족에게 복음을 전하고 말씀을 전할 수 있도록 문을 열어 주셨을 뿐만 아니라 다른 나라에서도 그렇게 할 수 있는 기회를 주셨습니다. 저는 말씀을 효과적으로 전파하는 데 언어가 중요하다는 것을 깨달았습니다. 따라서 열방에 하나님의 말씀을 전하기 위해 앞으로 6개월 동안 영어 실력을 향상시키는 데 힘쓰시기 바랍니다.

이 책은 다문화 환경에서 일하며 영어로 복음을 전하기 원하는 목회자, 선교사, 영적 지도자에게 추천합니다. 또한 영어 발음을 개선하고자 하는 모든 분들에게도 추천합니다. 또한 제2외국어로 사역해야 하는 여러 나라의 선교사들에게도 이 책은 귀중한 자료가 될 수 있습니다. 여기에 설명된 원칙은 모든 언어에 적용하여 발음을 향상시킬 수 있으며, 다양한 상황에서 자신 있게 말씀을 나누고 설교할 수 있게 해줍니다. 궁극적으로 이 책은 더 많은 사람들이 예수님의 복음을 듣고 믿음 안에서 성장하여 우리 주님이시자 구주이신 그리스도 예수의 명령대로 말씀을 전파하라는 사명을 완수하도록 돕는 것을 목표로 합니다.

목차

이 책의 사용방법

이 책을 통해 더 나은 영어 말하기, 특히 영어 설교를 위해 최대한의 효과를 얻으려면 다음 단계를 따르세요.

이 책의 목적 이해하기:

1. 이 책은 영어 문법이나 독해 기술을 가르치지 않습니다. 이러한 부분에 도움이 필요하다면 다른 자료를 활용하세요.

2. 이 책은 특히 하나님의 말씀을 전하기 위해 영어를 명확하게 말하는 방법을 향상시키는 데 초점을 맞추고 있습니다.

기간과 과정:

1. 각 파트마다 40 일씩, 총 120 일이 소요됩니다.

2. 며칠을 건너뛰면서 서두르지 마세요. 차근차근 단계를 밟아 영어 설교 실력을 향상하세요.

파트 1: 발음(1~40 일)

1. 매일 30 분 이상 모음과 자음 발음을 연습하세요.

2. 이미 모든 발음을 다 안다고 생각하고 건너뛰지 마세요.

3. QR 코드와 링크를 통해 제공되는 동영상 부분을 반복하여 보고 들어보세요. 반복해서 연습하는 것이 발음 향상의 핵심입니다.

4. 매주 5 일째 되는 날마다 복습을 통해 그 주에 배운 내용을 정리하세요.

2부: 스토리텔링(41~80 일차)

1.　단어 발음을 개선한 후, 문장을 연결하여 읽는 연습을 합니다.

2.　먼저 소리 내어 그 날의 분량을 읽고 그림과 연관 지어 읽은 다음 동영상을 보며 따라해 봅니다.

3.　동영상의 원어민을 따라 문장을 반복 연습합니다. 동영상이 너무 빠르면 속도를 늦춰서 천천히 발음해도 좋습니다.

4.　배운 내용을 기억하는 데 도움이 되도록 그림을 외우세요.

3부: 설교 준비 및 전달 (81-120 일)

1.　첫 20 일 동안은 설교 본문을 이해하고 동영상 없이 설교 원고를 작성하는 데 집중합니다.

2.　21~30 일차에는 설교 원고 작성을 마무리하는 데 도움이 되도록 동영상을 시청합니다.

3.　발음을 향상시키기 위해 설교원고를 소리 내어 읽는 연습을 합니다.

4.　마지막 10 일은 설교 전달력 향상에 집중합니다.

다음 단계:

- 이 책이 마무리 할 때쯤이면 자신 있게 영어로 설교할 수 있을 것입니다.

- 계속해서 복음을 전하고 배운 내용을 영어 설교에 적용하세요.

- 영어 말하기 능력을 배우고 성장하는 것을 멈추지 마세요.

Pronunciation

English Phonetic Alphabets

모음 (20):

1. Monophthongs:

   /iː/ - bee, team

   /ɪ/ - bit, fit

   /e/ - bed, red

   /æ/ - bat, man

   /ə/ - Agree, item, The schwa sound, a neutral vowel sound

   /ɑː/ - car, father

   /ɒ/ - hot, box

   /ɔː/ - saw, floor

   /ʊ/ - full, put

   /uː/ - moon, boot

   /ʌ/ - cup, mud

   /ɜː/ - Third

2. Diphthongs:

   /əʊ/ - go, soul

   /ai/ - nice, pie

   /aɪ/ - write, light

   /ɔɪ/ - boy, oil

/eɪ/ - day, rain

/ʊə/ - sure, pure

/ɪə/ - here, beer

/eə/ - Hair

자음 (24):

1. Stops:

    /p/ - pet, sip

    /b/ - big, rob

    /t/ - top, hat

    /d/ - dog, red

    /k/ - cat, kick

    /g/ - go, big

2. Fricatives:

    /f/ - fin, laugh

    /v/ - van, love

    /θ/ - thin, think

    /ð/ - then, this

    /s/ - see, sun

    /z/ - zoo, buzz

    /ʃ/ - ship, wish

    /tʃ/ -Chair, Church

/ʒ/ - measure, pleasure

/dʒ/ - Jeep, judge

3. Nasals:

/m/ - man, am

/n/ - no, win

/ŋ/ - sing, long

4. Liquids:

/l/ - lip, milk

/r/ - red, run

5. Semivowels:

/w/ - wet, win

/h/ - hat, hot

/j/- You

앞으로 40 일 동안 44 가지 영어 발음을 연습하여 영어 말하기 실력을 향상시켜 보세요. 영어 설교 실력을 향상하는 데 중요한 단계이므로 건너뛰지 마세요.

PART I: 발음 (40 DAYS)

Week 1 (Vowels 1)

Day 1

/iː/: Long i - bee, team, ease

오늘의 동영상을 시청하고 오늘의 부분을 최소 10 회 이상 연습하세요.
QR 코드를 스캔하세요.

Day 2

/ɪ/: Short i - bit, fit, his

오늘의 동영상을 시청하고 오늘의 부분을 최소 10 회 이상 연습하세요.
QR 코드를 스캔하세요.

Day 3

/e/: Short e - bed, red, then

/æ/: Short a - bat, man, act

오늘의 동영상을 시청하고 오늘의 부분을 최소 10 회 이상 연습하세요.
QR 코드를 스캔하세요.

Day 4

/ə/ - Agree, item, of, the schwa sound, a neutral vowel sound

영어에서 강세가 없는 음절에서 많이 나타나는 매우 짧고 중성적이며 편안한 모음 소리입니다. 오늘의 동영상을 시청하고 오늘의 부분을 최소 10 번 이상 연습하세요. QR 코드를 스캔하세요.

Day 5

/iː/ - bee, team, ease
/ɪ/ - bit, fit, his
/e/ - bed, red, then
/æ/ - bat, man, act
/ə/ - Agree, item, of

이번 주 수업을 복습해 봅시다! 오늘의 동영상을 시청하고 오늘 배운 부분을 최소 10 회 이상 연습하세요. QR 코드를 스캔하세요.

Week 2 (Vowels II)

Day 6

/ɑː/: Long A - car, father, art

오늘의 동영상을 시청하고 오늘 배운 부분을 최소 10 회 이상 연습하세요. QR 코드를 스캔하세요.

Day 7

/ɒ/: Short o - hot, box

오늘의 동영상을 시청하고 오늘 배운 부분을 최소 10 회 이상 연습하세요. QR 코드를 스캔하세요.

Day 8

/ɔː/: Long o - saw, floor, aught

오늘의 동영상을 시청하고 오늘 배운 부분을 최소 10 회 이상 연습하세요. QR 코드를 스캔하세요.

Day 9

/ʊ/: Short u - full, put, would

오늘의 동영상을 시청하고 오늘 배운 부분을 최소 10 회 이상 연습하세요. QR 코드를 스캔하세요.

Day 10

/ɑː/ - car, father, art

/ɒ/ - hot, box

/ɔː/ - saw, floor, aught

/ʊ/ - full, put, would

이번 주 수업을 복습해 봅시다! 오늘의 동영상을 시청하고 오늘 배운 부분을 최소 10 회 이상 연습하세요. QR 코드를 스캔하세요.

Week 3 (Vowels III)

Day 11

/uː/: Long u - moon, boot, who

오늘의 동영상을 시청하고 오늘 배운 부분을 최소 10 회 이상 연습하세요. QR 코드를 스캔하세요.

Day 12

/ʌ/ - cup, mud, must

오늘의 동영상을 시청하고 오늘 배운 부분을 최소 10 회 이상 연습하세요. QR 코드를 스캔하세요.

Day 13

/ɜ:/: Long er - Third, learn

오늘의 동영상을 시청하고 오늘 배운 부분을 최소 10 회 이상 연습하세요. QR 코드를 스캔하세요.

Day 14

/uː/ - moon, boot, who
/ʌ/ - cup, mud, must
/3ː/ - Third, learn

오늘의 동영상을 시청하고 오늘 배운 부분을 최소 10 회 이상 연습하세요. QR 코드를 스캔하세요.

Day 15

"Who would know aught of art, must learn, act, then take his ease."

이 문장에는 지금까지 배운 모음의 조합이 포함되어 있습니다. 오늘의 동영상을 시청하고 오늘의 부분을 최소 10 번 이상 연습하세요. QR 코드를 스캔하세요.

Week 4 (Vowels IV)

Day 16

/əʊ/ - go, soul
/ai/ - nice, pie

/əʊ/ 소리의 경우, 먼저 /ə/ 소리를 낸 다음 /ʊ/를 발음하기 위해 입을 둥글게 모으면서 발음하세요. 오늘의 동영상을 시청하고 오늘의 부분을 10 회 이상 연습하세요. QR 코드를 스캔하세요.

Day 17

/aɪ/ - write, light
/ɔɪ/ - boy, oil

오늘의 동영상을 시청하고 오늘의 부분을 10 회 이상 연습하세요. QR 코드를 스캔하세요.

Day 18

/eɪ/ - day, rain

/ʊə/ - sure, pure

오늘의 동영상을 시청하고 오늘의 부분을 10 회 이상 연습하세요. QR 코드를 스캔하세요.

Day 19

/ɪə/ - here, beer
/eə/ - Hair

오늘의 동영상을 시청하고 오늘의 부분을 10 회 이상 연습하세요. QR 코드를 스캔하세요.

Day 20

/əʊ/ - go, soul

/ai/ - nice, pie

/aɪ/ - write, light

/ɔɪ/ - boy, oil

/eɪ/ - day, rain

/ʊə/ - sure, pure

/ɪə/ - here, beer

/eə/ - Hair

이번 주 수업을 복습해 봅시다! 오늘의 동영상을 시청하고 오늘 배운 부분을 10 회 이상 연습하세요. QR 코드를 스캔하세요.

Week 5 (Consonants 1)

Day 21

/p/ - pet, sip
/b/ - big, rob

오늘의 동영상을 시청하고 오늘 배운 부분을 10 회 이상 연습하세요.
QR 코드를 스캔하세요.

Day 22

/t/ - top, hat
/d/ - dog, red

오늘의 동영상을 시청하고 오늘 배운 부분을 10 회 이상 연습하세요.
QR 코드를 스캔하세요.

Day 23

/k/ - cat, kick

오늘의 동영상을 시청하고 오늘 배운 부분을 10 회 이상 연습하세요. QR 코드를 스캔하세요.

Day 24

/g/ - go, big

오늘의 동영상을 시청하고 오늘 배운 부분을 10 회 이상 연습하세요.
QR 코드를 스캔하세요.

Day 25

/p/ - pet, sip

/b/ - big, rob

/t/ - top, hat

/d/ - dog, red

/k/ - cat, kick

/g/ - go, big

이번 주 수업을 복습해 봅시다! 오늘의 동영상을 시청하고 오늘 배운 부분을 10 회 이상 연습하세요. QR 코드를 스캔하세요.

Week 6 (Consonants 11)

Day 26

/f/ - fin, laugh
/v/ - van, love

오늘의 동영상을 시청하고 오늘 배운 부분을 10 회 이상 연습하세요.
QR 코드를 스캔하세요.

Day 27

/θ/ - thin, think

/ð/ - then, this

오늘의 동영상을 시청하고 오늘 배운 부분을 10 회 이상 연습하세요.
QR 코드를 스캔하세요.

Day 28

/s/ - see, sun

오늘의 동영상을 시청하고 오늘 배운 부분을 10회 이상 연습하세요. QR 코드를 스캔하세요.

Day 29

/z/ - zoo, buzz

오늘의 동영상을 시청하고 오늘 배운 부분을 10 회 이상 연습하세요.
QR 코드를 스캔하세요.

Day 30

/f/ - fin, laugh

/v/ - van, love

/θ/ - thin, think

/ð/ - then, this

/s/ - see, sun

/z/ - zoo, buzz

이번 주 수업을 복습해 봅시다! 오늘의 동영상을 시청하고 오늘 배운 부분을 10 회 이상 연습하세요. QR 코드를 스캔하세요.

Week 7 (Consonants III)

Day 31

/ʃ/ - ship, wish

/tʃ/ -Chair, Church

오늘의 동영상을 시청하고 오늘 배운 부분을 10 회 이상 연습하세요.
QR 코드를 스캔하세요.

Day 32

/ʒ/ - measure, pleasure

오늘의 동영상을 시청하고 오늘 배운 부분을 10 회 이상 연습하세요.
QR 코드를 스캔하세요.

Day 33

/dʒ/ - Jeep, judge

오늘의 동영상을 시청하고 오늘 배운 부분을 10 회 이상 연습하세요.
QR 코드를 스캔하세요.

Day 34

/m/ - man, am

/n/ - no, win

오늘의 동영상을 시청하고 오늘 배운 부분을 10 회 이상 연습하세요.
QR 코드를 스캔하세요.

Day 35

/ʃ/ - ship, wish

/tʃ/ -Chair, Church

/ʒ/ - measure, pleasure

/dʒ/ - Jeep, judge

/m/ - man, am

/n/ - no, win

이번 주 수업을 복습해 봅시다! 오늘의 동영상을 시청하고 오늘 배운 부분을 10 회 이상 연습하세요. QR 코드를 스캔하세요.

Week 8 (Consonants IV)

Day 36

/ŋ/ - sing, long

오늘의 동영상을 시청하고 오늘 배운 부분을 10 회 이상 연습하세요.
QR 코드를 스캔하세요.

Day 37

/l/ - lip, milk
/r/ - red, run

오늘의 동영상을 시청하고 오늘 배운 부분을 10 회 이상 연습하세요.
QR 코드를 스캔하세요.

Day 38

/w/ - wet, win

오늘의 동영상을 시청하고 오늘 배운 부분을 10 회 이상 연습하세요.
QR 코드를 스캔하세요.

Day 39

/h/ - hat, hot

/j/- You

오늘의 동영상을 시청하고 오늘 배운 부분을 10 회 이상 연습하세요.
QR 코드를 스캔하세요.

Day 40

/ŋ/ - sing, long

/l/ - lip, milk

/r/ - red, run

/w/ - wet, win

/h/ - hat, hot

/j/- You

이번 주 레슨을 복습해 보겠습니다. 오늘은 발음 향상을 위한 40 일간의 수업이 마무리되는 날입니다. 발음을 숙달했다면 다음 단계인 스토리텔링으로 넘어가세요. 더 많은 연습이 필요하다면 발음에 자신감이 생길 때까지 계속 연습하는 것이 좋습니다. 그 후에는 다음 단계로 넘어갈 수 있습니다. 오늘의 동영상을 시청하고 오늘의 부분을 10 회 이상 연습하세요. QR 코드를 스캔하세요.

Story Telling

PART II: 스토리텔링

(40 Days- C2C (Creation to Christ) Story)

이번 파트는 문장 말하기 연습입니다. 첫 번째 파트에서는 각 영어 문자, 모음, 자음을 말하는 방법을 배웠습니다. 이제 이를 사용하여 문장을 만들어 보세요. 하지만 문장이 서로 어떻게 연결되는지 이해하지 못하면 문장을 말하는 것만으로는 도움이 되지 않습니다. 가장 좋은 방법은 스토리텔링입니다. 스토리란 서로 의미가 있고 흐름이 있는 여러 문장을 묶은 것입니다. 또한 이 파트에서는 매우 중요한 이야기인 예수 그리스도의 복음을 스토리텔링으로 말하는 것을 배우게 됩니다. 이와 함께 스토리를 그림으로 그리는 방법도 배우게 되므로 시각적효과로 문장의 순서를 더 잘 기억하는 데 도움이 됩니다. 이 모든 것이 앞으로 40 일 동안 영어로 복음을 전하는 방법을 가르쳐 줄 것입니다. 이것은 영어로 설교를 작성하고 설교하는 방법을 배우기 전의 중요한 단계입니다. 그러니 이 부분을 건너뛰지 마시고 첫 번째 파트에서 했던 것처럼 매일 연습하세요. 자 그럼 함께 두번째 파트를 시작해 봅시다!

Week 9

Day 1 (Day 41)

Hello! I want to share an amazing story that changed my life.

동영상을 시청하면서 원어민이 말하는 문장을 5 번 이상 따라하면서 자유롭게 말할 수 있을 때까지 연습하세요. 동영상이 너무 빠른 경우 동영상을 일시 정지했다가 다시 재생하여 각 단어와 문장을 정확하게 발음할 수 있을 때까지 반복합니다.

QR 코드를 스캔하세요.

Day 2 (Day 42)

God existed by Himself even before the world began.
He is greater than all things, and He is the most powerful.
He is also the creator of all things.

동영상을 시청하고 원어민이 말하는 문장을 5 번 이상 따라하거나, 자신 있게 말할 수 있을 때까지 연습하세요. QR 코드를 스캔하여 동영상을 시청하세요.

Day 3 (Day 43)

God created beautiful angels to serve and worship Him in heaven.

He also created heaven and earth, sea and sea creatures, sun and moon, stars, birds in the sky, and all the plants and animals.

동영상을 시청하고 원어민이 말하는 문장을 5 번 이상 따라하거나, 자신 있게 말할 수 있을 때까지 연습하세요. QR 코드를 스캔하여 동영상을 시청하세요.

Day 4 (Day 44)

Lastly, He made man and woman in His image.
He let them enjoy the beautiful garden and
manage everything in the garden.
God commanded them to eat all the fruits in
the garden except the fruit from the tree in the
middle of the garden.

동영상을 시청하고 원어민이 말하는 문장을 5 번 이상 따라하거나, 자신
있게 말할 수 있을 때까지 연습하세요. QR 코드를 스캔하여 동영상을
시청하세요.

Day 5 (Day 45)

If they eat it, they will die.
They had a good relationship with God,
keeping His commands.

이번 주 내용을 복습해봅시다!

1. Hello! I want to share an amazing story that changed my life.
2. God existed by Himself even before the world began.
3. He is greater than all things, and He is the most powerful.
4. He is also the creator of all things.
5. God created beautiful angels to serve and worship Him in heaven.
6. He also created heaven and earth, sea and sea creatures, sun and moon, stars, birds in the sky, and all the plants and animals.
7. Lastly, He made man and woman in His image. He let them enjoy the beautiful garden and manage everything in the garden.

8. God commanded them to eat all the fruits in the garden except the fruit from the tree in the middle of the garden.
9. If they eat it, they will die.
10. They had a good relationship with God, keeping His commands.

동영상을 시청하고 원어민이 말하는 문장을 5번 이상 따라하거나, 자신 있게 말할 수 있을 때까지 연습하세요. QR 코드를 스캔하여 동영상을 시청하세요.

Week 10

Day 6 (Day 46)

Do you remember the angels God created?
The most beautiful and smart angel among them became proud and desired to be like God.

동영상을 시청하고 원어민이 말하는 문장을 5 번 이상 따라하거나, 자신 있게 말할 수 있을 때까지 연습하세요. QR 코드를 스캔하여 동영상을 시청하세요.

Day 7 (Day 47)

God expelled the proud angel and those who followed him from heaven.
The proud angel became Satan, and the others became demons.

동영상을 시청하고 원어민이 말하는 문장을 5 번 이상 따라하거나, 자신 있게 말할 수 있을 때까지 연습하세요. QR 코드를 스캔하여 동영상을 시청하세요.

Day 8 (Day 48)

**On a particular day, Satan seduced the
woman to eat the fruit God forbade.
She ate the fruit and gave it to her husband.
He ate it as well.
They ate what God commanded them not to
eat. Disobedience is a sin.**

동영상을 시청하고 원어민이 말하는 문장을 5 번 이상 따라하거나, 자신
있게 말할 수 있을 때까지 연습하세요. QR 코드를 스캔하여 동영상을
시청하세요.

Day 9 (Day 49)

God has no sin, and He cannot be with
their sin of disobedience.
Therefore, they were separated from
God and expelled from the garden.
The relationship with God was broken.

동영상을 시청하고 원어민이 말하는 문장을 5 번 이상 따라하거나, 자신
있게 말할 수 있을 때까지 연습하세요. QR 코드를 스캔하여 동영상을
시청하세요.

Day 10 (Day 50)

They had to die for their sin and go to hell to suffer eternal punishment.

We all sin, and our relationship with God is broken.

We will also be punished in hell forever.

이번 주 내용을 복습해봅시다!

1. **Do you remember the angels God created?**

2. The most beautiful and smart angel among them became proud and desired to be like God.

3. God expelled the proud angel and those who followed him from heaven.

4. The proud angel became Satan, and the others became demons.

5. On a particular day, Satan seduced the woman to eat the fruit God forbade.

6. She ate the fruit and gave it to her husband. He ate it as well.

7. They ate what God commanded them not to eat. Disobedience is a sin.

8. God has no sin, and He cannot be with their sin of disobedience.

9. Therefore, they were separated from God and expelled from the garden.

10. The relationship with God was broken.

11. They had to die for their sin and go to hell to suffer eternal punishment.

12. We all sin, and our relationship with God is broken.
13. We will also be punished in hell forever.

동영상을 시청하고 원어민이 말하는 문장을 5 번 이상 따라하거나, 자신 있게 말할 수 있을 때까지 연습하세요. QR 코드를 스캔하여 동영상을 시청하세요.

Week 11

Day 11 (Day 51)

As time went by, there were more people in this world. God loved them and wanted to restore his relationship with them. But people had to stay away from sin to restore their relationship with God, who has no sin.

동영상을 시청하고 원어민이 말하는 문장을 5 번 이상 따라하거나, 자신 있게 말할 수 있을 때까지 연습하세요. QR 코드를 스캔하여 동영상을 시청하세요.

Day 12 (Day 52)

10

**So, God gave them the Ten
Commandments to help them stay away
from sin, but no one could keep the
commandments perfectly.
God is sinless and pure, so He had to
punish the sins of his people.**

동영상을 시청하고 원어민이 말하는 문장을 5 번 이상 따라하거나, 자신 있게 말할 수 있을 때까지 연습하세요. QR 코드를 스캔하여 동영상을 시청하세요.

Day 13 (Day 53)

But God loved them, so He showed a way for people to be forgiven of their sins.

The way is to bring a clean animal to God whenever one sins, then to repent of the sin and to slay the animal on behalf of the person.

When God sees the blood of the animal, He forgives the sin of the person. The Bible says, "Without the shedding of blood, there is no forgiveness of sins." (Hebrews 9:22) This is how God shows us to be forgiven of our sins.

동영상을 시청하고 원어민이 말하는 문장을 5 번 이상 따라하거나, 자신 있게 말할 수 있을 때까지 연습하세요. QR 코드를 스캔하여 동영상을 시청하세요.

Day 14 (Day 54)

But as time went by, people did not genuinely repent of their sins.
They ritualistically killed and shed the blood of animals.
God was not pleased with the blood of animals.
The relationship with God could not be restored through keeping the commandments and animal sacrifice.

동영상을 시청하고 원어민이 말하는 문장을 5 번 이상 따라하거나, 자신 있게 말할 수 있을 때까지 연습하세요. QR 코드를 스캔하여 동영상을 시청하세요.

Day 15 (Day 55)

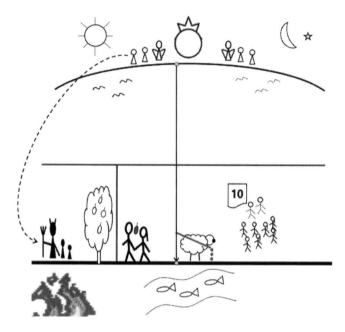

Nevertheless, God still loved his people, and He had compassion for people who could not solve their sins through their efforts.

So, He sent Jesus, the ultimate way of restoration God prepared a long time ago.

1. As time went by, there were more people in this world.
2. God loved them and wanted to restore his relationship with them.
3. But people had to stay away from sin to restore their relationship with God, who has no sin.
4. So God gave them the Ten Commandments to help them stay away from sin, but no one could keep the commandments perfectly.
5. God is sinless and pure, so He had to punish the sins of his people.
6. But God loved them, so He showed a way for people to be forgiven of their sins.
7. The way is to bring a clean animal to God whenever one sins, then to repent of the sin and to slay the animal on behalf of the person.
8. When God sees the blood of the animal, He forgives the sin of the person.

9. The Bible says, "Without the shedding of blood, there is no forgiveness of sins." (Hebrews 9:22)

10. This is how God shows us to be forgiven of our sins.

11. But as time went by, people did not genuinely repent of their sins.

12. They ritualistically killed and shed the blood of animals.

13. God was not pleased with the blood of animals.

14. The relationship with God could not be restored through keeping the commandments and animal sacrifice.

15. Nevertheless, God still loved his people, and He had compassion for people who could not solve their sins through their efforts.

16. So He sent Jesus, the ultimate way of restoration God prepared a long time ago.

동영상을 시청하고 원어민이 말하는 문장을 5번 이상 따라하거나, 자신 있게 말할 수 있을 때까지 연습하세요. QR 코드를 스캔하여 동영상을 시청하세요.

Week 12

Day 16 (Day 56)

**Who is Jesus? Jesus is
God's only Son, a wise teacher, and perfect
without sin. Powerful and performs miracles.**

동영상을 시청하고 원어민이 말하는 문장을 5 번 이상 따라하거나, 자신 있게 말할 수 있을 때까지 연습하세요. QR 코드를 스캔하여 동영상을 시청하세요.

Day 17 (Day 57)

He calmed the ocean with His word while He and His disciples were in a storm.
He has the power to rule over nature.
He also cast out demons.
He is greater than any evil power.

동영상을 시청하고 원어민이 말하는 문장을 5 번 이상 따라하거나, 자신 있게 말할 수 있을 때까지 연습하세요. QR 코드를 스캔하여 동영상을 시청하세요.

Day 18 (Day 58)

He fed the 5000 with two fish and five pieces of bread.
He knows and meets our needs with His power.

동영상을 시청하고 원어민이 말하는 문장을 5 번 이상 따라하거나, 자신 있게 말할 수 있을 때까지 연습하세요. QR 코드를 스캔하여 동영상을 시청하세요.

Day 19 (Day 59)

He raised a person who was dead for 4 days.
Jesus defeats death.
Jesus proved he was God's Son through these miracles.

동영상을 시청하고 원어민이 말하는 문장을 5 번 이상 따라하거나, 자신 있게 말할 수 있을 때까지 연습하세요. QR 코드를 스캔하여 동영상을 시청하세요.

Day 20 (Day 60)

He is also the Good Shepherd.
He never leaves us alone.
He leads us to the right path and protects
us from evil.

이번 주 내용을 복습해봅시다!

1. God's only Son, a wise teacher, and
   perfect without sin.
2. Powerful and performs miracles.
3. He calmed the ocean with His word
   while He and His disciples were in a
   storm.
4. He has the power to rule over nature.
5. He also cast out demons.

6. He is greater than any evil power.
7. He fed the 5000 with two fish and five pieces of bread.
8. He knows and meets our needs with His power.
9. He raised a person who was dead for 4 days.
10. Jesus defeats death.
11. Jesus proved he was God's Son through these miracles.
12. He is also the Good Shepherd.
13. He never leaves us alone.
14. He leads us to the right path and protects us from evil.

동영상을 시청하고 원어민이 말하는 문장을 5번 이상 따라하거나, 자신 있게 말할 수 있을 때까지 연습하세요. QR 코드를 스캔하여 동영상을 시청하세요.

Week 13

Day 21 (Day 61)

Many people followed Jesus when he was on earth, but many hated and envied him.
They wanted to kill him.
Jesus gave his body to them.

동영상을 시청하고 원어민이 말하는 문장을 5 번 이상 따라하거나, 자신 있게 말할 수 있을 때까지 연습하세요. QR 코드를 스캔하여 동영상을 시청하세요.

Day 22 (Day 62)

His hands and feet were nailed to the cross.
He shed his blood and died in excruciating pain.
The cross was meant for the worst criminals during that time.

동영상을 시청하고 원어민이 말하는 문장을 5 번 이상 따라하거나, 자신 있게 말할 수 있을 때까지 연습하세요. QR 코드를 스캔하여 동영상을 시청하세요.

Day 23 (Day 63)

By the way, why did sinless Jesus have to die on the cross? It is because Jesus is the perfect sacrifice God prepared to forgive the sins of everyone in this world.

동영상을 시청하고 원어민이 말하는 문장을 5 번 이상 따라하거나, 자신 있게 말할 수 있을 때까지 연습하세요. QR 코드를 스캔하여 동영상을 시청하세요.

Day 24 (Day 64)

**The wages of sin are death, so we sinners
are to die, but Jesus became the sacrifice
and died on the cross in our place.
God said there is no forgiveness without
shedding blood.
So God saw the blood of Jesus on the
cross and forgave our sins.**

동영상을 시청하고 원어민이 말하는 문장을 5 번 이상 따라하거나, 자신
있게 말할 수 있을 때까지 연습하세요. QR 코드를 스캔하여 동영상을
시청하세요.

Day 25 (Day 65)

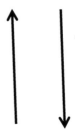

Jesus died and rose again in three days.
He showed himself to many people and
ascended into heaven.
He promised to come back to judge the
world.

이번 주 내용을 복습해봅시다!

1. Many people followed Jesus when he
   was on earth, but many hated and envied
   him.
2. They wanted to kill him.
3. Jesus gave his body to them.
4. His hands and feet were nailed to the
   cross.

5. He shed his blood and died in excruciating pain.

6. The cross was meant for the worst criminals during that time.

7. By the way, why did sinless Jesus have to die on the cross?

8. It is because Jesus is the perfect sacrifice God prepared to forgive the sins of everyone in this world.

9. The wages of sin are death, so we sinners are to die, but Jesus became the sacrifice and died on the cross in our place.

10.   God said there is no forgiveness without shedding blood.

11. So God saw the blood of Jesus on the cross and forgave our sins.

12. Jesus died and rose again in three days.

13. He showed himself to many people and ascended into heaven.

14. He promised to come back to judge the world.

동영상을 시청하고 원어민이 말하는 문장을 5 번 이상 따라하거나, 자신 있게 말할 수 있을 때까지 연습하세요. QR 코드를 스캔하여 동영상을 시청하세요.

Week 14

Day 26 (Day 66)

When He was on earth, He told the story of a father who had two sons.
On a particular day, the second son came to his father and asked for his inheritance.
The father gave it to him, and the son left for a faraway country.

동영상을 시청하고 원어민이 말하는 문장을 5 번 이상 따라하거나, 자신 있게 말할 수 있을 때까지 연습하세요. QR 코드를 스캔하여 동영상을 시청하세요.

Day 27 (Day 67)

He squandered all the money he had.
He worked in a pig farm to survive yet he was still hungry.
When he was at rock bottom, he thought about his father's home in abundance.
The son decided to go back to his father's home.

동영상을 시청하고 원어민이 말하는 문장을 5번 이상 따라하거나, 자신 있게 말할 수 있을 때까지 연습하세요. QR 코드를 스캔하여 동영상을 시청하세요.

Day 28 (Day 68)

Ever since the son left home, his father has been waiting for his son's return. When he saw his son coming home, he ran to him and hugged him with gladness.

동영상을 시청하고 원어민이 말하는 문장을 5 번 이상 따라하거나, 자신 있게 말할 수 있을 때까지 연습하세요. QR 코드를 스캔하여 동영상을 시청하세요.

Day 29 (Day 69)

But the son asked for forgiveness and told his father to use him as a servant. The father forgave the son and welcomed him as his son, not as a servant.

동영상을 시청하고 원어민이 말하는 문장을 5번 이상 따라하거나, 자신 있게 말할 수 있을 때까지 연습하세요. QR 코드를 스캔하여 동영상을 시청하세요.

Day 30 (Day 70)

We are all like the second son.
We also left God the Father and lived
with sin as we wanted.
Because of the sin, we were separated
from God, and we were going to suffer in
hell forever.
But God, the Father, still waits for us to
repent and turn to Him.

이번 주 내용을 복습해봅시다!

1. When He was on earth, He told the story
   of a father who had two sons.
2. On a particular day, the second son came
   to his father and asked for his
   inheritance.
3. The father gave it to him, and the son left
   for a faraway country.
4. He squandered all the money he had.

5. He worked in a pig farm to survive yet he was still hungry.

6. When he was at rock bottom, he thought about his father's home in abundance.

7. The son decided to go back to his father's home.

8. Ever since the son left home, his father has been waiting for his son's return.

9. When he saw his son coming home, he ran to him and hugged him with gladness.

10. But the son asked for forgiveness and told his father to use him as a servant.

11. The father forgave the son and welcomed him as his son, not as a servant.

12. We are all like the second son.

13. We also left God the Father and lived with sin as we wanted.

14. Because of the sin, we were separated from God, and we were going to suffer in hell forever.

15. But God, the Father, still waits for us to repent and turn to Him.

동영상을 시청하고 원어민이 말하는 문장을 5 번 이상 따라하거나, 자신 있게 말할 수 있을 때까지 연습하세요. QR 코드를 스캔하여 동영상을 시청하세요.

Day 31 (Day 71)

**Do you want to go back to God, the Father?
Jesus said, "I am the way, truth, and life. No one
comes to the Father except through me" (John
14:6).**

동영상을 시청하고 원어민이 말하는 문장을 5 번 이상 따라하거나, 자신
있게 말할 수 있을 때까지 연습하세요. QR 코드를 스캔하여 동영상을
시청하세요.

Day 32 (Day 72)

?

**Jesus is the only way to go back to God,
the Father.
Do you want to go to God through Jesus?**

동영상을 시청하고 원어민이 말하는 문장을 5번 이상 따라하거나, 자신
있게 말할 수 있을 때까지 연습하세요. QR 코드를 스캔하여 동영상을
시청하세요.

Day 33 (Day 73)

If so, you must acknowledge your sin first and believe that Jesus died on the cross for your sins and that He rose from the dead.

동영상을 시청하고 원어민이 말하는 문장을 5 번 이상 따라하거나, 자신 있게 말할 수 있을 때까지 연습하세요. QR 코드를 스캔하여 동영상을 시청하세요.

Day 34 (Day 74)

Confess with your mouth that Jesus is
the Savior who saved you from your sins,
and He is the Lord of your life.
Then your sins will be forgiven, and you
can go to God.

동영상을 시청하고 원어민이 말하는 문장을 5 번 이상 따라하거나, 자신 있게 말할 수 있을 때까지 연습하세요. QR 코드를 스캔하여 동영상을 시청하세요.

Day 35 (Day 75)

Do you want to believe and confess that Jesus is your Lord and Savior?

동영상을 시청하고 원어민이 말하는 문장을 5번 이상 따라하거나, 자신 있게 말할 수 있을 때까지 연습하세요. QR 코드를 스캔하여 동영상을 시청하세요.

Week 16

Day 36 (Day 76)

Thank you! Repeat after me as I pray.
"Jesus, I am a sinner.

동영상을 시청하고 원어민이 말하는 문장을 5 번 이상 따라하거나, 자신 있게 말할 수 있을 때까지 연습하세요. QR 코드를 스캔하여 동영상을 시청하세요.

Day 37 (Day 77)

**I believe that Jesus is God's perfect
sacrifice and that He died on the cross
for me, and He rose from the dead."
Forgive my sins and come into my heart
to be my Lord and Savior.**

동영상을 시청하고 원어민이 말하는 문장을 5 번 이상 따라하거나, 자신
있게 말할 수 있을 때까지 연습하세요. QR 코드를 스캔하여 동영상을
시청하세요.

Day 38 (Day 78)

**Guide me until I go to heaven.
In Jesus' name, I prayed. Amen"
Congratulations! God promised that all
who receive Him, who believe in His
name, would have the right to become
children of God" (John 1:12).**

동영상을 시청하고 원어민이 말하는 문장을 5 번 이상 따라하거나, 자신 있게 말할 수 있을 때까지 연습하세요. QR 코드를 스캔하여 동영상을 시청하세요.

Day 39 (Day 79)

**Now, you have become His child
according to His promise.
Your sins are forgiven, and your
relationship with God is restored.**

동영상을 시청하고 원어민이 말하는 문장을 5번 이상 따라하거나, 자신 있게 말할 수 있을 때까지 연습하세요. QR 코드를 스캔하여 동영상을 시청하세요.

Day 40 (Day 80)

Do you love your family?
God also loves your family and wants
them to come to Him.
Would you share this good news with
your family and friends?

이번 주 내용을 복습해 봅시다!

1. Thank you! Repeat after me as I pray.
2. "Jesus, I am a sinner.
3. I believe that Jesus is God's perfect
   sacrifice and that He died on the cross
   for me, and He rose from the dead."
4. Forgive my sins and come into my heart
   to be my Lord and Savior.
5. Guide me until I go to heaven.
6. In Jesus' name, I prayed. Amen"
7. Congratulations! God promised that all
   who receive Him, who believe in His

name, would have the right to become children of God" (John 1:12).

8. Now, you have become His child according to His promise.

9. Your sins are forgiven, and your relationship with God is restored.

10. Do you love your family?

11. God also loves your family and wants them to come to Him.

12. Would you share this good news with your family and friends?

동영상을 시청하고 원어민이 말하는 문장을 5 번 이상 따라하거나, 자신 있게 말할 수 있을 때까지 연습하세요. QR 코드를 스캔하여 동영상을 시청하세요.

C2C Full-Script

"Hello! I want to share an amazing story that changed my life.

God existed by Himself even before the world began. He is greater than all things, and He is the most powerful.

He is also the creator of all things.

God created beautiful angels to serve and worship Him in heaven.

He also created heaven and earth, sea and sea creatures, sun and moon, stars, birds in the sky, and all the plants and animals.

Lastly, He made man and woman in His image. He let them enjoy the beautiful garden and manage everything in the garden.

God commanded them to eat all the fruits in the garden except the fruit from the tree in the middle of the garden. If they eat it, they will die. They had a good relationship with God, keeping His commands.

Do you remember the angels God created? The most beautiful and smart angel among them became proud and desired to be like God.

God expelled the proud angel and those who followed him from heaven. The proud angel became Satan, and the others became demons.

On a particular day, Satan seduced the woman to eat the fruit God forbade.

She ate the fruit and gave it to her husband. He ate it as well.

They ate what God commanded them not to eat. Disobedience is a sin.

God has no sin, and He cannot be with their sin of disobedience.

Therefore, they were separated from God and expelled from the garden. The relationship with God was broken.

They had to die for their sin and go to hell to suffer eternal punishment.

We all sin, and our relationship with God is broken. We will also be punished in hell forever.

As time went by, there were more people in this world. God loved them and wanted to restore his relationship with them.

But people had to stay away from sin to restore their relationship with God, who has no sin.

So God gave them the Ten Commandments to help them stay away from sin, but no one could keep the commandments perfectly.

God is sinless and pure, so He had to punish the sins of his people.

But God loved them, so He showed a way for people to be forgiven of their sins.

The way is to bring a clean animal to God whenever one sins, then to repent of the sin and to slay the animal on behalf of the person. When God sees the blood of the animal, He forgives the sin of the person.

The Bible says, "Without the shedding of blood, there is no forgiveness of sins." (Hebrews 9:22) This is how God shows us to be forgiven of our sins.

But as time went by, people did not genuinely repent of their sins. They ritualistically killed and shed the blood of animals. God was not pleased with the blood of animals. The relationship with God could not be restored through keeping the commandments and animal sacrifice.

Nevertheless, God still loved his people, and He had compassion for people who could not solve their sins through their efforts.

So He sent Jesus, the ultimate way of restoration God prepared a long time ago.

Who is Jesus?
Jesus is;

1. God's only Son, a wise teacher, and perfect without sin.

2. Powerful and performs miracles.

1) He calmed the ocean with His word while He and His disciples were in a storm. He has the power to rule over nature.

2) He also cast out demons. He is greater than any evil power.

3) He fed the 5000 with two fish and five pieces of bread. He knows and meets our needs with His power.

4) He raised a person who was dead for 4 days. Jesus defeats death.

Jesus proved he was God's Son through these miracles.

He is also the Good Shepherd. He never leaves us alone. He leads us to the right path and protects us from evil.

Many people followed Jesus when he was on earth, but many hated and envied him. They wanted to kill him.

Jesus gave his body to them. His hands and feet were nailed to the cross. He shed his blood and died in excruciating pain. The cross was meant for the worst criminals during that time.

By the way, why did sinless Jesus have to die on the cross?

It is because Jesus is the perfect sacrifice God prepared to forgive the sins of everyone in this world.

The wages of sin are death, so we sinners are to die, but Jesus became the sacrifice and died on the cross in our place.

God said there is no forgiveness without shedding blood. So God saw the blood of Jesus on the cross and forgave our sins.

Jesus died and rose again in three days. He showed himself to many people and ascended into heaven. He promised to come back to judge the world.

When He was on earth, He told the story of a father who had two sons.

On a particular day, the second son came to his father and asked for his inheritance. The father gave it to him, and the son left for a faraway country.

He squandered all the money he had. He worked in a pig farm to survive yet he was still hungry.

When he was at rock bottom, he thought about his father's home in abundance. The son decided to go back to his father's home.

Ever since the son left home, his father has been waiting for his son's return. When he saw his son coming home, he ran to him and hugged him with gladness.

But the son asked for forgiveness and told his father to use him as a servant. The father forgave the son and welcomed him as his son, not as a servant.

We are all like the second son. We also left God the Father and lived with sin as we wanted.

Because of the sin, we were separated from God, and we were going to suffer in hell forever. But God, the Father, still waits for us to repent and turn to Him.

Do you want to go back to God, the Father?

Jesus said, "I am the way, truth, and life. No one comes to the Father except through me" (John 14:6).

Jesus is the only way to go back to God, the Father.

Do you want to go to God through Jesus? If so, you must acknowledge your sin first and believe that Jesus died on the cross for your sins and that He rose from the dead.

Confess with your mouth that Jesus is the Savior who saved you from your sins, and He is the Lord of your life. Then your sins will be forgiven, and you can go to God.

Do you want to believe and confess that Jesus is your Lord and Savior? Thank you! Repeat after me as I pray.

"Jesus, I am a sinner. I believe that Jesus is God's perfect sacrifice and that He died on the cross for me, and He rose from the dead."

Forgive my sins and come into my heart to be my Lord and Savior. Guide me until I go to heaven. In Jesus' name, I prayed. Amen"

Congratulations! God promised that all who receive Him, who believe in His name, would have the right to become children of God" (John 1:12).

Now, you have become His child according to His promise. Your sins are forgiven, and your relationship with God is restored.

Do you love your family? God also loves your family and wants them to come to Him.

Would you share this good news with your family and friends?"

Sermon Script

PART III (설교준비 및 전달)

Week 17 (Interpretation 1)

Day 1 (Day 81)

30 분 동안 기도하며 하나님의 말씀을 통해 하나님의 음성을 들어보세요.

Day 2 (Day 82)

– 마가복음 5:1-20 을 ESV 번역본으로 세 번 이상 읽으세요.

"1They came to the other side of the sea, to the country of the Gerasenes. 2And when Jesus had stepped out of the boat, immediately there met him out of the tombs a man with an unclean spirit. 3He lived among the tombs. And no one could bind him anymore, not even with a chain, 4for he had often been bound with shackles and chains, but he wrenched the chains apart, and he broke the shackles in pieces. No one had the strength to subdue him. 5Night and day among the tombs and on the mountains he was always crying out and cutting himself with stones. 6And when he saw Jesus from afar, he ran and fell down before him. 7And crying out with a loud voice, he said, "What have you to do with me, Jesus, Son of the Most High God? I adjure you by God, do not torment me." 8For he was saying to him, "Come out of the man, you unclean spirit!" 9And Jesus asked him, "What is your name?" He replied, "My name is Legion, for we are many." 10And he begged him earnestly not to send them out of the country. 11Now a great herd of pigs was feeding there on the hillside, 12and they begged him, saying, "Send us to the pigs; let us enter them." 13So he gave them permission. And the unclean spirits came out and entered the pigs; and the herd, numbering about two thousand, rushed down the steep bank into the sea and drowned in the sea.

14The herdsmen fled and told it in the city and in the country. And people came to see what it was that had happened. 15And they came to Jesus and saw the demon-possessed man, the one who had had the legion, sitting there, clothed and in his right mind, and they were afraid. 16And those who had seen it described to them what had happened to the demon-possessed man and to the pigs. 17And they began to beg Jesus to depart from their region.18As he was getting into the boat, the man who had been possessed with demons begged him that he might be with him. 19And he did not permit him but said to him, "Go home to your friends and tell them how much the Lord has done for you, and how he has had mercy on you." 20And he went away and began to proclaim in the Decapolis how much Jesus had done for him, and everyone marveled."

Day 3 (Day 83)

주어진 본문을 해석하려면, 적어도 세 번 이상 읽고 다음 질문에 답하세요(이 책 혹은 다른 노트에 작성하세요).

1) 이 본문의 키워드는 무엇인가요? 반복되는 단어가 있나요?

2) 그 단어의 의미는 무엇인가요?

3) 본문의 주제는 무엇인가요?

Day 4 (Day 84)

1) 키워드는 무엇인가요?

-Unclean spirits (1-13v)
-Demon-possessed man (14-20v)

2) 키워드의 의미를 찾습니다. 단어의 원어와 의미를 찾으려면 biblehub.com 과 같은 성경 앱을 참조하세요.

-<u>Unclean spirits</u>: ′더러운 영′(τò πνεῦμα τò ἀκάθαρτον)은 죄로 오염된 잘못된 영을 의미하며, ′성령′(πνεύματι)은 세상과는 다른 영을 의미합니다.

*Legion (군대) (v9): 로마 군대의 한 사단(6,826 명)=더러운 영이 많다는 뜻입니다.
-<u>Demon possessed</u> 귀신들림 (δαιμονιζομένῳ): 귀신에 힘에 억눌려 지배를 받고 있는 것을 뜻합니다.

Day 5 (Day 85)

본문의 주제를 찾습니다. (본문에서 하나의 큰 아이디어를 찾는 것이 중요합니다. 설교에 너무 많은 아이디어가 포함되어 있으면 이해하기 어렵고 산만해집니다).

본문을 다시 읽고 주요 아이디어를 파악합니다.

주요 아이디어(주제)

-예수님은 죄로 더럽혀진 더러운 영을 쫓아내고 귀신 들린 사람을 귀신의 지배에서 해방시키셨습니다.

Week 18 (Interpretation 11)

Day 6 (Day 86)

부제는 무엇인가요? (주제를 찾은 후, 이를 뒷받침하는 부제를 찾을 수 있습니다.)

1-5 절을 읽고 주제를 뒷받침하는 부제를 찾아보세요.

(1-5v) They came to the other side of the sea, to the country of the Gerasenes. And when Jesus had stepped out of the boat, immediately there was a man with an unclean spirit. He lived among the tombs. And no one could bind him anymore, not even with a chain, for he had often been bound with shackles and chains, but he wrenched the chains apart, and he broke the shackles in pieces. No one had the strength to subdue him. Night and day among the tombs and on the mountains, he was always crying out and cutting himself with stones.

(1–5v) **Jesus met the man with unclean spirits.** 4 Conditions of the man with an unclean spirit.
- Living in the tomb

- No one could stop him.
- Breaking all chains
- Crying out and cutting himself with stones every day and night

Day 7 (Day 87)

6-13절을 읽고 부제를 찾아보세요.

(6-13v) And when he saw Jesus from afar, he ran and fell before him. And crying out with a loud voice, he said, "What have you to do with me, Jesus, Son of the Most High God? I adjure you by God; do not torment me." For he was saying to him, "Come out of the man, you unclean spirit!" And Jesus asked him, "What is your name?" He replied, "My name is Legion, for we are many." And he begged him earnestly not to send them out of the country. 11 Now a great herd of pigs was feeding there on the hillside, and they begged him, saying, "Send us to the pigs; let us enter them." So he permitted them. And the unclean spirits came out and entered the pigs, and the herd, numbering about two thousand, rushed down the steep bank into the sea and drowned in the sea.

(6-13v) Jesus cast out unclean spirits.
-The man fell before him and begged, "Don't torture me."
-Jesus commanded the unclean spirit to come out of the man, and it identified itself as "Legion" (consisting of 6000 evil spirits).
-The spirits begged Jesus to send them into a nearby herd of pigs, which he did.
-The pigs then ran into a lake and drowned.

Day 8 (Day 88)

14-20 절을 읽고 부제를 찾으세요.

The herdsmen fled and told it in the city and the country. And people came to see what it was that had happened. And they came to Jesus and saw the demon-possessed man, the one who had had the legion, sitting there, clothed and in his right mind, and they were afraid. And those who had seen it described to them what had happened to the demon-possessed man and the pigs. And they began to beg Jesus to depart from their region. As he was getting into the boat, the man who had been possessed by demons begged him that he might be with him. And he did not permit him but said to him, "Go home to your friends and tell them how much the Lord has done for you and how he has had mercy on you." And he went away and began to proclaim in the Decapolis how much Jesus had done for him, and everyone marveled.

(14-20v) Jesus changed the man possessed by a demon.

-He begged to follow Jesus.

-Jesus instructed him to share what He had done.

Day 9 (Day 89)

메인 아이디어 (주제) 와 서브 아이디어 (부제)들을 함께 정리해 봅시다.

Main Idea (주제) (Mark 5:1–20): ***-Jesus cast out unclean spirits tainted by sin and freed the demon-possessed man from the control of a demon.***

Sub Ideas (부제):

- Jesus met the man with unclean spirits. (1-5v)
- Jesus cast out unclean spirits. (6-13v)
- Jesus changed the man possessed by a demon. (14-20v)

Day 10 (Day 90)

성경 전체의 중요한 주제를 아는 것은 매우 중요합니다.

성경 전체의 주제는 무엇인가요? 그리스도 예수입니다.

"이에 모세와 및 모든 선지자의 글로 시작하여 모든 성경에 쓴바 자기 (그리스도)에 관한 것을 자세히 설명하시니라"
누가복음 24:27

"구약성경은 예수님이 완성하신 이야기를 들려줄 뿐만 아니라 예수님이 이루신 약속을 선언합니다." 크리스토퍼 라이트

메인 아이디어나 서브 아이디어에 '그리스도'가 언급되어 있는지 확인하세요.

구약 성경 본문에서도 그리스도를 찾고 설교할 수 있습니다.

예를 들어, 사무엘상 17:41-53 에서 골리앗은 다윗과 하나님을 모욕하지만 결국 다윗이 골리앗을 물리치고 이스라엘이 블레셋을 물리치는 승리로 이끌게 됩니다. 이 이야기는 궁극적인

적인 마귀를 물리치신 예수님의 궁극적인 승리를 예표한 것으로
볼 수 있습니다.

Week 19 (Outline and illustration)

Day 11 (Day 91)

설교 개요는 어떻게 작성하나요?

1. 설교제목을 정합니다.

예) Jesus the demon caster, the power of Jesus, etc.

제 제목은 'nature (본성)'입니다.

2. 부제를 더욱 간결하고 명확하게 만듭니다.

Jesus met the man with unclean spirits. (1-5v)

->**Nature of Evil (악의 본성)**

Jesus cast out unclean spirits. (6-13v)

->**Nature of God (하나님의 본성)**

Jesus changed the man with unclean spirits. (14-20v)

->**Nature of Change (변화의 본성)**

3. 설교주제와 부제를 일관성있게 작성합니다.

Sermon Title (주제): Nature (본성)

- **Nature of Evil (1–5v) -악의 본성**
- **Nature of God (6-13v) -하나님의 본성**
- **Nature of Change (14-20v)- 변화의 본성**

4. 부제에 내용을 연결합니다.

Nature of Evil (1–5v)- 악의 본성

-Evil is <u>more powerful</u> than human control (uncontrollable, destructible power). -악은 인간보다 훨씬 강하다.

-Evil <u>does not love</u> God (kneel before God, but "don't torture me").- 악은 하나님을 사랑하지 않는다.

Nature of God (6-13v)- 하나님의 본성

-Jesus is <u>more powerful</u> than evil. (Legion was defeated.)- 예수님은 악보다 훨씬 강하시다.

-Jesus is <u>loving</u> (coming through the storm to the worst place to save this man).-예수님은 사랑이시다.

Nature of Change (14-20v)- 변화의 본성

-Change is <u>more powerful</u> than the former condition (sitting and dressed).-변화된 삶은 이전보다 훨신 강하다.

-Change promotes love, for Jesus is <u>loving</u> (the first missionary to the Gentiles).- 예수님이 사랑이시기에 변화된 삶은 사랑하는 삶이다.

Day 12 (Day 92)

1. 정리한 내용을 가지고 설교 개요를 작성합니다.

Nature of Evil (1–5v)

The devil is more **powerful** than humans.
The evil does not **love** God.

Nature of God (6-13v)

Jesus is more **powerful** than evil.
Jesus is **loving**.

Nature of Change (14-20v)

Change is more **powerful** than the former condition.
Change promotes **love** for Jesus.

2. 도입과 결론을 붙입니다.

도입 ("nature (본성)"에 관한 도입내용을 작성하세요.)

Body

Nature of Evil (1–5v)

The devil is more powerful than humans.

The evil does not love God.

Nature of God (6-13v)

Jesus is more powerful than evil.

Jesus is loving.

Nature of Change (14-20v)

Change is more powerful than the former condition.

Change promotes love for Jesus.

결론 ("Nature (본성)"에 관한 결론을 도출하세요.)

Day 13 (Day 93)

좋은 예시 만들기(I): 좋은 예시는 상승(+, 긍정적인 단어와 문장)과 하강(-, 부정적인 단어와 문장)이 있는 역동적인 예시입니다.

예를 들면 다음과 같습니다:

1. Key Word: "Light"

We are in darkness (-)

Sin is darkness, and we are in sin. (-)

There is the eternal death for our sin (-)

Jesus is the light. (+)

Jesus shines (+) in the darkness. (-)

Jesus came to us. (+)

2. 적용 점 만들기

We need to stop being in the darkness.

We need to come to Jesus, who is the light.

We need to share Jesus, who is the light.

3. 이번 주에 적용할 일 예시

Spend less time on your smartphone.

Spend more time reading the Bible every day.

Share the message of Jesus, who brings light, at least twice a week.

Day 14 (Day 94)

좋은 예시 만들기 **(II)**

1. **"nature (본성)"**을 강조하는 단어 찾기

    1) Nature of Evil (1–5v)

The devil is more **powerful** than humans.

The evil does not **love** God.

    2) Nature of God (6-13v)

Jesus is more **powerful** than evil.

Jesus is **loving**.

    3) Nature of Change (14-20v)

Change is more **powerful** than the former condition.

Change promotes **love** for Jesus.

2. 주제어와 관련된 단어 선택

-Catchy (주의를 끌만한 단어)

-Common (보편적으로 알려진 단어)

e.g.) "Nature" --> *"Nature of **Robots** (로봇)*

Day 15 (Day 95)

좋은 예시 만들기 (III)

1. 선택된 단어를 +,-로 묘사합니다.

(e.g.) Nature of "Robot" (로봇의 본성)

-Artificial, no life (-): 인공적인, 생명이 없는 (-)

-Smart, no break (+): 쉬지 않고 일할 수 있는 똑똑한 (+)

-It can take human jobs in 10 years. (-): 10 년 안에 인간이 직장을 잃어버릴 수 있음. (-)

-confusion between humans and robots (-): 인공지능 로봇과 인간과의 차이점이 점점 없어짐.

--> What differentiates humans from robots? 그렇다면 무엇이 인간을 로봇과 다르게 하는가?

    --> Human Nature (Love)(+): 인간의 본성 (사랑) (+)

2.   예시문을 작성합니다.

(예) God created humans differently from robots. God is love. Humans can love. Robots can't.

Humans and robots are different. Likewise, God and evil are different.

People who met God and who didn't are different as well.

We need to know the nature of God, evil, and change in the human heart.

3.   예시를 어디에 둘지 결정합니다.

-Introduction (도입)

-Body (본문)

-Conclusion (결론)

예: 저는 설교의 도입부에 이 예시를 넣었습니다.

"These days, we hear a lot about artificially intelligent robots. A study shows that in 10 years, lots of jobs will disappear because of these robots. They can read and think like humans and work much more than humans. Jobs like cashier, editor, construction work, and even high-level work like lawyer and doctor will disappear because the robots can do all of them. Is it exciting?"

No! It is scary because a lot of people will lose their jobs! The bigger problem is that a lot of people will be confused about the difference between humans and robots! Just like the bumper sticker saying "My dog is better than your kid," there will be a bumper sticker saying "My robot is better than your wife, your husband, or you!" It is coming pretty soon!

But don't be confused! There is a clear difference between humans and robots! What differentiates a human from a robot? It is "**human nature.**" One of the human natures is this: humans can love! Robots cannot love! Only humans can love! A robot can take over your job, but it cannot take over your nature. **That nature distinguishes us from robots.** Today, I want to share with you about nature and the three big distinguishing natures: The nature _of evil, the nature of God, and the nature of change!_

Week 20 (Writing a Sermon Script)

Day 16 (Day 96)

좋은 적용을 만드는 방법(앤디 스탠리의 다섯 가지 논리적 적용의 흐름): 적용에 다섯 가지 부분이 모두 포함되어 있다면 설교를 위한 강력한 적용이 될 수 있습니다.

- 무엇을 적용하는가? (명확성)

- 왜 (동기) 그러한 적용을 해야 하는가?

- 적용을 하기 위해 어떤 대가를 치러야 하는가(헌신)?

- 어떤 모습으로 적용하는가 (비전)?

- 적용을 할 때 어떤 영향을 미칠 것인가(결과)?

아래에서 적용의 좋은 사례와 나쁜 사례를 살펴보고 어떻게 다른지 살펴보세요.

안 좋은 적용 사례

'Jesus commanded us to make disciples. Our church vision is disciple-making. So let's make disciples."

좋은 적용 사례

'Disciples are the ones who follow Christ always. (clarification: 명확성). We must make disciples because Jesus commanded us to do so (motivation: 동기). We must live intentionally every day to make disciples (commitment: 헌신). Disciple-making will happen at your home, school, and workplace (vision:비전). So God will multiply His disciples through your disciple-making life (result: 결과).'

Day 17 (Day 97)

설교를 역동적으로 만드는 방법
1) 주제를 반복해서 말합니다.
2) 역동적인 개념을 사용합니다: 부정(-), 긍정(+).

아래에서 좋은 예와 나쁜 예를 살펴보고 어떻게 다른지 살펴보세요.

나쁜 예:

Disciple-**making is important!** Jesus said, "Go and make disciples." If you don't do it, you are disobeying God. It will be really bad. So we should go and make disciples!

좋은 예:

Disciple-making is Jesus' command, which means all Christians must do! You may have lots of excuses not to make **disciples**. You are busy at work, and you don't know much about the Bible, so you have nothing to say. You are **too lazy to** (-)meet and **disciple** anyone. But what if your non-believing friends **die tonight? (-)** That poor soul will face God's judgment and will die in eternal hellfire.

How **painful (-)** it will be for your friends. How **selfish (-)** it will be for you. But God is the TV, **Savior (+).** He can save your friend. God is the **Lord (+)**. He commands you to **disciple** your friend. you! **Disciple-making** is God's **heart** (+) and command. So do not waste your time, and **make disciples**!

Day 18 (Day 98)

설교에서 문장을 만드는 방법

V.I.P. 문장 만들기.
- (V) Visual: 눈앞에 펼쳐지는 다채로운 이야기처럼 청중의 마음속에 생생한 이미지를 그려주는 문장.
- (I) Interesting: 듣는 사람이 호기심을 가지고 귀를 기울이게 만드는 매력적인 문장.
- (P) Personal: 자신의 경험과 관심사에 맞춘 문장으로, 강의가 아닌 대화처럼 느껴지는 문장.

주어진 문장에서 V.I.P. 문장을 만들어 보세요: **"Disciples are the ones who always follow Jesus."**

V (Visual): **Disciples** open up the Bible before ***sunrise, during the sunshine, or after the sunset***. **Disciples** bring one more ***coffee to their coworkers*** and say, "How are you? I was praying for you yesterday." **Disciples** sit next to a lonely person at the ***lunch table,*** listen to their family issues, and share the story of Jesus, who cared for two sisters who lost their brother.

I (Interesting): Steve is your ***Twitter follower.*** Mary is your ***Facebook friend***. The problem is that you don't even know them! Disciples are not like that! Disciples follow Jesus, and Jesus is their friend. They know Jesus. Jesus loves them! Disciples and Jesus love each other!

P (Personal): Disciples follow Jesus all the time. ***I used*** to be a disciple of rock music. **I** listened to rock music every day. **I kept** taking pictures of musicians all the time. But after **I became a** disciple of Jesus, **I** began to listen to sermons and read the Bible each day.

좋은 예: Martin Luther King Jr. (I Have a Dream speech)

- I have a dream that one day on the red hills of Georgia, the sons of former slaves and the sons of former slave owners will be able to sit down together at a table of brotherhood.
- I have a dream that one day even the state of Mississippi, a desert state sweltering with the heat of injustice and oppression, will be transformed into an oasis of freedom and justice.
- I have a dream that my four children will one day live in a nation where they will not be judged by the color of their skin but by the content of their character.

Day 19 (Day 99)

설교원고 초안작성 법

1. 첫번째 초안(그냥 쓰기!)

2. 두 번째 초안: 전체 원고를 읽고 점검합니다("그리스도"가 중심이 되고, 성경적으로 견고하며, 성경에 충실하고, "본성"이라는 주제가 강조되고, 논리적인 흐름이 있는지). 중복되는 문장을 잘라냅니다.

3. 세 번째 초안: 단락이 역동성 (+,-)을 가지고 있는지 확인

4. 네 번째 초안: (V.I.P.)문장으로 작성

Day 20 (Day 100)

다양한 색상 (형광펜)으로 주요 요점을 강조 표시합니다.

예) The evil devil **does not love God.** Well, some may say, *I can control (??)* those evil forces in my heart. I got over lust, hatred, and all these things! I am a good person. I am not evil! Well, how about this? Evil is not only uncontrollable power but also a lack of love for God. 6-7v) And when he saw Jesus from afar, he ran and fell down before him. 7And crying out with a loud voice, he said, "What have you to do with me, Jesus, Son of the Most High God? I adjure you by God, do not torment me." Even with this evil nature, he came to Jesus and fell on his knees in front of him. That's good! That's worship and praise!! Right? How can an evil person worship Jesus? Is it possible? Look at verse 7! Instead of saying, "Jesus, I love you!" or "I trust in you alone," the man said, "What do you want with me? "Don't torture me!" Do you hear "Don't bother me! Leave me alone! I have no business with you, Jesus." **The evil one does not have any love for Jesus. That is the nature of evil**! They may come to bow down to Him and have lots of theological knowledge about Jesus, but they do not want to have any relationship with Him.

Week 21 (Writing and Reading a Full Script 1)

Day 21 (Day 101)

전체 원고의 일부를 작성하고 읽어보겠습니다.

These days, we hear a lot about artificially intelligent robots. A study shows that in 10 years, lots of jobs will disappear because of these robots. They can read and think like humans and work much more than humans. Jobs like cashier, editor, construction work, and even high-level work like lawyer and doctor will disappear because the robots can do all of them. Is it exciting? No! It is scary because a lot of people will lose their jobs! The bigger **problem is that a lot of people will be confused about the difference between humans and robots!** Just like the bumper sticker saying "My dog is better than your kid," there will be a bumper sticker saying "My robot is better than your wife, your husband, or you!" It is coming pretty soon!

But don't be confused! There is a clear difference between humans and robots! What differentiates a human from a robot? It is **"human nature."** One of the human natures is this: humans can love! Robots cannot love! Only humans can love! A robot can take over your job, but it cannot take over your nature. That nature distinguishes us from robots. Today, I want to share with you about nature and the three big distinguishing natures: The nature **of evil, the nature of God, and the nature of change!**

원어민이 원고를 읽는 것을 여러 번 듣고 따라하세요. QR 코드를 스캔하여 동영상을 시청하세요.

Day 22 (Day 102)

전체원고의 일부를 쓰고 읽어보세요.

1. **Nature of Evil**: (1-2v) They came to the other side of the sea, to the country of the Gerasenes.*ᵃ* **2**And when Jesus*ᵇ* had stepped out of the boat, immediately there met him out of the tombs a man with an unclean spirit.

Last week, we learned that Jesus and the disciples were crossing a huge lake, but there was a huge hurricane. The disciples were fishermen but could not control the storm, but Jesus calmed the storm. It was in the evening, and right after this, they landed on the land. It must be night, and **they have not slept yet**. But instead of staying in a hotel or being welcomed by people in the land, guess what? A demon-possessed man was coming. You might say, "Oh, boy, a demon-possessed man right after the storm? *Give me a break!!* What kind of mission trip is this? What's going on?" Not a good day! **But Jesus is going to show His power as He did in the lake. Now, what is the nature of evil?**

원어민이 원고를 읽는 것을 여러 번 듣고 따라하세요. QR 코드를 스캔하여 동영상을 시청하세요.

Day 23 (Day 103)

전체 원고의 일부를 쓰고 읽어보세요.

1) The evil <u>is more powerful than human control.</u> This man had a very severe condition. 3v) He lived among the tombs. And no one could bind him anymore, not even with a chain, Lonely man! He lived in the tombs! **No home!** No one was taking care of him, and **no one could control him**. How lonely he could be! But he had a **strange and strong power**. 4v) for he had often been bound with shackles and chains, but he wrenched the chains apart, and he broke the shackles in pieces. No one had the strength to subdue

him. *He must be nominated as the "most powerful man" of the year*! He is almost like a **Hulk in a Hollywood** movie. The metal chains and the irons were broken by him. He was <u>uncontrollable! He is Superman! No one could control him.</u>

Isn't that wonderful power and freedom? Isn't that what we want? Power and freedom? But when we have those, do you think we **will be happy?** Was he happy? No! 5v) Night and day among the tombs and on the mountains he was always crying out and cutting himself with stones. He did not enjoy the "Hulk"-like power. Instead, he cried out all the time and cut himself. **The power of evil is so strong,** but **it destroys everything! That is the nature of evil!** The power of evil is not how scary it looks, like in the scary movie, but rather *how "uncontrollable" and "destructible"* it is! **"Lust, pride, fear, jealousy, hatred, and all the names of problems in our minds" are uncontrollable and destructible.** They are *true and powerful evils!* Evil is not about scary ghosts in the movie. **It is about the destructive sinful nature in us!**

원어민이 원고를 읽는 것을 여러 번 듣고 따라하세요. QR 코드를 스캔하여 동영상을 시청하세요.

Day 24 (Day 104)

전체 원고의 일부를 쓰고 읽어보세요.

-Evil does not love God: Well, some may say, *I can control (??) over* those evil forces in my heart. I got over lust, hatred, and all these things! I am a good person. I am not evil! Well, how about this**? Evil is not only uncontrollable power but also a lack of love for God.** 6-7v) And when he saw Jesus from afar, he ran and fell down before him. 7And crying out with a loud voice, he said, "What have you to do with me, Jesus, Son of the Most High God? I adjure you by God, do not torment me." Even with this evil nature, **he came to Jesus and fell on his knees in front of him.** That's good! That's worship and praise!! Right? How can an evil person worship Jesus? Is it possible? Look at verse 7! Instead of saying, "Jesus, I love you!" or "I trust in you alone," the man said, "I adjure you by God, do not torment me." Do you hear "Don't bother me! Leave me alone! I have no business with you, Jesus." The evil **one does not have any love for Jesus. That is the nature of evil**! They may come to bow down to Him and have lots of theological knowledge about Jesus, but they do not want to have any relationship with Him.

원어민이 원고를 읽는 것을 여러 번 듣고 따라하세요. QR 코드를 스캔하여 동영상을 시청하세요.

Day 25 (Day 105)

전체 원고의 일부를 쓰고 읽어보세요.

This power of evil permeates all around the world. People are addicted to some sort of power (*drug, sex, money, political power, fame, etc.*) that is **uncontrollable, destructible, and leads to a lack of love for God.** This evil power was so big that no one could control it. **<u>But there is one who can control it: God!</u>** Let's look at the second point: <u>the nature of God.</u>

1. **Nature of God**: (8-9v) For Jesus had said to him, "For he was saying to him, "Come out of the man, you unclean spirit!" **9**And Jesus asked him, "What is your name?" He replied, "My name is Legion, for we are many."

<u>Jesus is more powerful than evil power.</u> Evil is more powerful than humans, but God is more powerful than evil. Jesus simply spoke to the man, "<u>Come out of this man, you unclean spirit!</u>" And then he asked a weird question. "***What is your name?***" The purpose of asking a question is to

show how powerful the evil spirit was in the man. The evil spirit answered, "My name is Legion, for we are many." Not just one or two spirits, but a lot. How many? The Legion **is a Roman military term. It refers to 4–6,000 soldiers** who could fight in the battle. Therefore, the "evil spirits" in the man were a huge, strong army, and that was why he was uncontrollable. Jesus just **fought with the storm** on the lake, which even fishermen could not control. Jesus is fighting here with a **huge army of evil spirits that** even the whole region cannot control. It was a big fight! 10v) And he begged him earnestly not to send them out of the country. Who won the fight? Jesus! Look at the word "begged." An evil spirit was begging Jesus. That means the evil spirit has already been defeated! Here are *thousands of evil spirits and a super-tired Jesus*. But **the fight was not competitive!** Many people think Jesus and the evil spirits have equal power! No! **Jesus is superior to any other spirit!** Any other things? **Even nature obeys, and the evil spirits subdue Jesus**! Evil power is stronger than human power, but Jesus is stronger than evil power. **That supreme power is the nature of God. But not just the power; God is love. The supreme love is the nature of God.**

원어민이 원고를 읽는 것을 여러 번 듣고 따라하세요. QR 코드를
스캔하여 동영상을 시청하세요.

Week 22 (Writing and Reading of a Full Script 11)

Day 26 (Day 106)

전체원고의 일부를 쓰고 읽어보세요.

<u>Jesus is loving.</u> (11-13v) "Now a great herd of pigs was feeding there on the hillside, **12**and they begged him, saying, "Send us to the pigs; let us enter them." **13**So he gave them permission. And the unclean spirits came out and entered the pigs; and the herd, numbering about two thousand, rushed down the steep bank into the sea and drowned in the sea." Well, do you see love in these verses? Can you guess what kind of place Jesus and the disciples were? Look at what kind of animals there are: **pigs (11v)! This is a gentile land!** Jewish people did not have "pigs." Why? <u>OT law labels pigs as "unclean" animals.</u> They did not eat the pigs, did not sacrifice the pigs either. **It is just "unclean."** ***<u>So the fact that they have "a large herd of pigs" means that they are not Jewish people</u>***. The place was, in fact, outside of Jewish Palestine. **They are gentiles**. So here, Jesus is in the gentile place with an "unclean spirit" and an "unclean animal." The worst place he could be. He did not even have a rest. But regardless of the facts and knowing everything, **He came here to save this poor gentile man**!

원어민이 원고를 읽는 것을 여러 번 듣고 따라하세요. QR 코드를 스캔하여 동영상을 시청하세요.

Day 27 (Day 107)

전체원고의 일부를 쓰고 읽어보세요.

The demons requested to go to the pigs, and Jesus allowed them, then they went into the pigs and rushed down to the lake. Not just one or two, but **2,000 pigs died!** *Jesus sent the "unclean spirit" with the "unclean animal" to save this one man!* More than the thousand lives of the pig, Jesus cared for the life of the "one" gentile man. **Jesus' love for man is more powerful than the evil one!** For the one lost sheep, Jesus would leave the 99 sheep behind to look for the one lost. **To save the "one" soul, Jesus would go anywhere!** Whether it is an "unclean," "uncontrollable," or "**destructive**" place and people, **Jesus would not spare His precious life on the "<u>unclean, uncontrollable, destructive</u>" cross and the tomb! That is the love of God!** That is my love for you!! **<u>Jesus is more powerful than the evil one, but unlike the unloving evil spirit, Jesus is full of love for us!</u> Power and love!** They are the nature of God! Let's look at the last one: the nature of change.

원어민이 원고를 읽는 것을 여러 번 듣고 따라하세요. QR 코드를 스캔하여 동영상을 시청하세요.

Day 28 (Day 108)

전체원고의 일부를 쓰고 읽어보세요.

1. **Nature of Change**: (14–15v) The herdsmen fled and told it in the city and in the country. And people came to see what it was that had happened. <u>15</u>And they came to Jesus and saw the demon-possessed^c man, the one who had had the legion, sitting there, clothed and in his right mind, and they were afraid.

Change is more powerful than the former condition. After all this, the man was changed! Look at how the man was changed. <u>1) **He was sitting!**</u> That is a miracle! Well, we are all sitting here, but he was not! Day and night, he was wandering off, crying out, and cutting himself. Now, he does not have to do that anymore. He is quietly sitting for the first time in his life! And <u>2) **he is dressed!**</u> That is a miracle! We are all dressed up here, but he was not. He was naked and undignified. But he is dressed. ***<u>Being dressed means having an identity.</u>*** He belongs to a community. He did not even have his name. His name used to be "<u>Legion, the army of evil spirits,</u>" and no one wanted to hang out. But **he has a new identity now**. We still don't know his name, but <u>at least he is dressed</u>. **New...changed identity with dignity, experiencing the power of Jesus!**

원어민이 원고를 읽는 것을 여러 번 듣고 따라하세요. QR 코드를 스캔하여 동영상을 시청하세요.

Day 29 (Day 109)

전체원고의 일부를 쓰고 읽어보세요.

When Jesus saves us, **He gives us a new identity with dignity as the children of God**. We used to be slaves to evil spirits, controlled by them. But because of Jesus, we are **clothed with His righteousness**. We **belong to His community, the church, and the Kingdom of God**! But the people were not so excited about this change. Instead of rejoicing, the man became changed; <u>they were afraid.</u> (16-17v) And those who had seen it described to them what had happened to the demon-possessed man and to the pigs. <u>17</u>And they began to beg Jesus^d to depart from their region. Just like the **evil spirits**, they *did not want to have any relationship with Jesus*. "**Just leave us alone!**" They are still evil! **They cared more about their business loss—pigs—than** the man. **No love!** They are still evil!

원어민이 원고를 읽는 것을 여러 번 듣고 따라하세요. QR 코드를 스캔하여 동영상을 시청하세요.

Day 30 (Day 110)

전체원고의 일부를 쓰고 읽어보세요.

Change promotes love for Jesus. (18v) As he was getting into the boat, the man who had been possessed with demons begged him that he might be with him. But the man was trying to follow Jesus! **He used to beg, "Jesus, leave me alone. Don't torture me." But here, he is begging to follow anywhere he goes**. He did not love Jesus, but __now he loves Jesus__! 19-20v) Jesus did not let him, but said, "And he did not permit him but said to him, "Go home to your friends and tell them how much the Lord has done for you, and how he has had mercy on you." **20**And he went away and began to proclaim in the Decapolis how much Jesus had done for him, and everyone marveled. __Interestingly, Jesus did not allow it this time.__ But He said, "**I am your Lord**! Do not follow me;

instead, go back to your people (gentile) and tell them about what I have done for you! What **love and mercy** I have shown to you!" **He used to say, "Don't let me leave here!'** But here he obeyed Jesus and went outside. *He went away and went to Decapolis, the gentile territory (outside of Jewish Palestine), to share what God had done for him!* People were amazed. Even before Paul, **he was the first missionary to Gentiles! Jesus' love for him changed him and made him obey what Jesus said.**

Whatever evil nature you have, uncontrollable, destructible sin you are experiencing in your life now, trust the nature of the Lord, who is more powerful and loving than the nature of evil inside of you! He will change you! He will change your nature! *You will love Him and follow Him wherever He is and sends you.* Come and experience His power and love!

원어민이 원고를 읽는 것을 여러 번 듣고 따라하세요. QR 코드를 스캔하여 동영상을 시청하세요.

Week 23 (How to deliver a sermon)

Day 31 (Day 111)

설교자의 태도는 어떠해야 하나요?

1.   **말씀에 대한 갈망:** 첫째, 설교자의 태도가 중요합니다. 설교자는 하나님의 말씀을 간절히 사모해야 합니다. 설교가 지루한 일상이 되거나 매주 하는 부담이 된다면 그것은 훌륭한 사역이 될 수 없습니다. 하나님의 말씀에 대한 열망은 말씀을 진정으로 갈망하는 마음에서 자연스럽게 우러나야 합니다. 따라서 설교자는 항상 하나님의 말씀에 굶주려 있어야 합니다. 시편 119:97 에 언급된 것처럼 설교자는 하나님의 말씀의 단맛을 경험하고 매일 말씀을 갈망해야 합니다.

2.   **하나님과의 친밀함:** 둘째, 하나님의 말씀에 대한 갈망은 자연스럽게 하나님과의 친밀한 관계에서 비롯되어야 합니다. 매일 주님과 동행하는 것이 설교의 기초입니다. 설교는

비즈니스나 프레젠테이션이 아니라 하나님과의 일상적인 관계를 반영합니다. 친밀한 관계는 설교자의 기본 태도가 되어야 합니다.

3.   **회중을 돌봄:** 마지막으로, 설교자는 회중을 진정으로 돌봐야 합니다. 회중에 대한 사랑이 없다면 설교는 그 목적을 잃게 됩니다. 설교의 주요 청중은 회중입니다. 따라서 설교자는 회중에 대한 사랑이 커져야 합니다. 설교의 목적은 이 분야에서 최고의 설교자가 되기 위한 자기 홍보가 아니라 회중에게 삶을 변화시키는 메시지를 전달하는 것입니다. 설교자가 환상적인 메시지를 전달하더라도 회중이 영향을 받거나 변화되지 않는다면 그것은 유용하지 않습니다. 설교자는 회중을 위해 설교한다는 목적이 분명해야 합니다.

Day 32 (Day 112)

다이나믹 톤(I)

설교 중에는 설교를 흥미롭게 만들기 위해 음색을 바꿀 수 있습니다. 모노톤, 업톤, 다운톤, 하이톤의 네 가지 소리가 있습니다.

1. 모노톤 (설명) ─────────────

모노톤은 평평하고 변하지 않는 어조로 말하는 것을 말합니다. (예) "하나님의 백성이 이집트에서 나와 광야에서 살고 있었습니다. 낮에는 덥고 밤에는 추운 사막이었습니다."

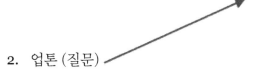

2. 업톤 (질문) ──────

업톤은 문장 끝에서 목소리가 올라가는 것을 말하며, 질문을 할 때 자주 사용합니다. (예) 그럼 사제들은 왜 항상 예복을 입어야 하나요? 사제들은 원하는 옷을 자유롭게 입을 수 있나요? 그냥 편한 옷을 입으면 안 될까요? 저처럼 청바지를 입으면 안 되나요?

Day 33 (Day 113)

다이나믹톤 (II)

3. 다운업톤 (비교)

다운업 톤은 나쁜 것을 좋은 것과 비교할 때 사용합니다. 나쁜 것에 대해 이야기할 때는 말의 분위기가 떨어지고, 좋은 것에 대해 이야기할 때는 말의 분위기가 올라갑니다. (예) 당신은 세상에서 가난합니다. (−) 하지만 당신은 천국의 궁전에 있습니다! (+) 당신은 나라를 잃었습니다. (−) 그러나 당신은 거룩한 나라라고 불립니다! (+) 당신은 사람들에게 버림받았습니다. (−) 그러나 당신은 하나님의 선택을 받았습니다. (+)

4. 하이톤 (강조)

하이톤은 중요한 요점을 계속 강조할 때 사용합니다. 다른 단어나 문장에 비해 더 크게 말하거나 높은 음조로 말함으로써 각 단어가

더 중요하게 들리게 합니다. (예) 당신은 선택된 백성, 왕 같은 제사장, 거룩한 나라, 특별한 소유입니다. 요컨대, 하나님은 "너는 아름답단다.   너는   거룩하단다.   그리고   너는   나에게 특별하단다" 라고 우리에게 말씀하십니다.

도입부 (모노톤 + 업톤)

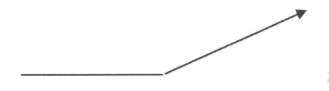

본문 (업톤 + 다운업톤)

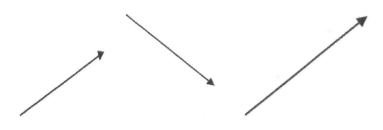

클라이맥스 (하이톤)

결론 (모노톤 + 업톤)

Day 34 (Day 114)

1. 눈 맞추기

- 원고를 5 번 이상 읽으세요!

- 원고를 머릿속으로 시각화하세요.

- 원고를 보지 않고 리허설을 하세요! 이렇게 하면 청중과 100% 눈을 맞추는 데 도움이 되고 자신감을 얻을 수 있습니다.

- 또한 청중의 눈을 너무 오래 응시하지 마세요. 대신 예배당 중앙을 가끔씩 바라보세요.

2. **제스처**

- 설교할 때는 손짓을 사용하는 것이 중요하지만 손가락으로 사람들을 가리키는 것은 피하세요.

- 부드러운 손동작을 사용하고 큰 제스처는 피하세요.

- 미소를 짓는 것도 중요하지만 지나치게 크게 웃는 것은 피하세요.

- 감정을 표현하는 것은 좋지만 강단에서 너무 많이 울먹이지 않도록 합니다.

- 열정을 가지고 설교하되, 몸을 움직이거나 '아' 또는 '음'과 같은 필러 단어를 사용하는 등의 매너리즘은 피하세요.

3.　　　**설교 시간 및 길이**

- 주일 아침 설교의 경우 25-40 분
- 수련회 및 부흥회의 경우 1 시간-1 시간 30 분
- 너무 빠르지도 느리지도 않은 적당한 속도여야 합니다.

Day 35 (Day 115)

마치는 말

- 설교를 준비하면서 매일 2 시간 이상 기도하세요. 이렇게 하면 마음을 준비하고 설교하는 동안 힘을 주시는 성령님께 의지하는 데 도움이 됩니다.

-항상 그리스도께 집중하세요. 자신이나 다른 사람에 대해 설교하지 않도록 주의하고, 대신 그리스도가 누구이신지, 그분이 하신 일에 대해 설교하세요.

- 주님과 그분의 말씀을 사랑하고 여러분이 설교하는 사람들을 사랑하세요. 주님과 그분의 말씀에 대한 사랑이 설교를 포함하여 여러분이 하는 모든 일의 기초가 되도록 하세요.

- 설교를 정직하게 준비하여 설교하는 말씀을 따르고 순종하도록 하세요. (에스라 7:10)

- 마지막으로, 때와 장소를 가리지 않고 주님에 대한 확신을 가지고 설교하세요. (디모데후서 4:2)

Week 24 (Rehearse your sermon)

Day 36 (Day 116)

여러분의 설교가 성령의 인도하심을 받도록 한 시간 이상 기도하세요!

Day 37 (Day 117)

전체 원고를 읽으세요 (부록 참조)

Day 38 (Day 118)

원고를　　머릿속으로　　시각화　　합니다.　　설교를
녹화합니다(비디오 또는 오디오). 그리고 시청하세요.

Day 39 (Day 119)

가족들 앞에서 설교 연습해 보세요.

Day 40 (Day 120)

친구 앞에서 설교 연습해 보세요. 그리고 피드백을
받습니다.

Week 25

지난 24 주 동안 배운 모든 내용을 복습하세요.

-발음

-스토리텔링 (C2C)

-설교 준비 및 발표

부록

Full Sermon Script

Mark 5:1-20 "Nature"

These days, we hear a lot about artificially intelligent robots. A study shows that in 10 years, lots of jobs will disappear because of these robots. They can read and think like humans and work much more than humans. Jobs like cashier, editor, construction work, and even high-level work like lawyer and doctor will disappear because the robots can do all of them. Is it exciting? No! It is scary because a lot of people will lose their jobs! The bigger **problem is that a lot of people will be confused about the difference between humans and robots!** Just like the bumper sticker saying "My dog is better than your kid," there will be a bumper sticker saying "My robot is better than your wife, your husband, or you!" It is coming pretty soon!

But don't be confused! There is a clear difference between humans and robots! What differentiates a human from a robot? It is **"human nature."** One of the human natures is this: humans can love! Robots cannot love! Only humans can love! A robot can take over your job, but it cannot take over your nature. That nature distinguishes us from robots. Today, I want to share with you about nature and the three big distinguishing natures: The nature **of evil, the nature of God, and the nature of change!**

2. **Nature of Evil**: (1-2v) They came to the other side of the sea, to the country of the Gerasenes.*a* **2**And when Jesus*b* had stepped out of the boat, immediately there met him out of the tombs a man with an unclean spirit.

Last week, we learned that Jesus and the disciples were crossing a huge lake, but there was a huge hurricane. The disciples were fishermen but could not control the storm, but Jesus calmed the storm. It was in the evening, and right after this, they landed on the land. It must be night, and **they have not slept yet**. But instead of staying in a hotel or being welcomed by people in the land, guess what? A demon-possessed man was coming. You might say, "Oh, boy, a demon-possessed man right after the storm? *Give me a break!!* What kind of mission trip is this? What's going on?"

Not a good day! **But Jesus is going to show His power as He did in the lake. Now, what is the nature of evil?**

1) The evil is more powerful than human control. This man had a very severe condition. 3v) He lived among the tombs. And no one could bind him anymore, not even with a chain, Lonely man! He lived in the tombs! **No home!** No one was taking care of him, and **no one could control him**. How lonely he could be! But he had a **strange and strong power**. 4v) for he had often been bound with shackles and chains, but he wrenched the chains apart, and he broke the shackles in pieces. No one had the strength to subdue him. *He must be nominated as the "most powerful man" of the year*! He is almost like a **Hulk in a Hollywood** movie. The metal chains and the irons were broken by him. He was uncontrollable! He is Superman! No one could control him.

Isn't that wonderful power and freedom? Isn't that what we want? Power and freedom? But when we have those, do you think we **will be happy?** Was he happy? No! 5v) Night and day among the tombs and on the mountains he was always crying out and cutting himself with stones. He did not enjoy the "Hulk"-like power. Instead, he cried out all the time and cut himself. **The power of evil is so**

strong, but **it destroys everything! That is the nature of evil!** The power of evil is not how scary it looks, like in the scary movie, but rather *how "uncontrollable" and "destructible"* it is! **"Lust, pride, fear, jealousy, hatred, and all the names of problems in our minds" are uncontrollable and destructible.** They are *true and powerful evils!* Evil is not about scary ghosts in the movie. **It is about the destructive sinful nature in us!**

-Evil does not love God: Well, some may say, *I can control (??) over* those evil forces in my heart. I got over lust, hatred, and all these things! I am a good person. I am not evil! Well, how about this? **Evil is not only uncontrollable power but also a lack of love for God.** 6-7v) And when he saw Jesus from afar, he ran and fell down before him. 7And crying out with a loud voice, he said, "What have you to do with me, Jesus, Son of the Most High God? I adjure you by God, do not torment me." Even with this evil nature, **he came to Jesus and fell on his knees in front of him.** That's good! That's worship and praise!! Right? How can an evil person worship Jesus? Is it possible? Look at verse 7! Instead of saying, "Jesus, I love you!" or "I trust in you alone," the man said, "I adjure you by God, do not torment me." Do you hear "Don't bother me!

Leave me alone! I have no business with you, Jesus." The evil **one does not have any love for Jesus. That is the nature of evil**! <u>They may come to bow down to Him and have lots of theological knowledge about Jesus, but they do not want to have any relationship with Him.</u>

This power of evil permeates all around the world. People are addicted to some sort of power (*drug, sex, money, political power, fame, etc.*) that is **uncontrollable, destructible, and leads to a lack of love for God.** This evil power was so big that no one could control it. **<u>But there is one who can control it: God!</u>** Let's look at the second point: <u>the nature of God.</u>

2. **Nature of God**: (8-9v) For Jesus had said to him, "For he was saying to him, "Come out of the man, you unclean spirit!" **9**And Jesus asked him, "What is your name?" He replied, "My name is Legion, for we are many."

<u>Jesus</u> <u>is more powerful than evil power.</u> Evil is more powerful than humans, but God is more powerful than evil. Jesus simply spoke to the man, "<u>Come out of this man, you unclean spirit!</u>" And then he asked a weird question. "***What***

is your name?" The purpose of asking a question is to show how powerful the evil spirit was in the man. The evil spirit answered, "My name is Legion, for we are many." Not just one or two spirits, but a lot. How many? The Legion **is a Roman military term. It refers to** <u>4–6,000 soldiers</u> who could fight in the battle. Therefore, the "<u>evil spirits</u>" in the man were a <u>huge, strong army, and that was why he was uncontrollable.</u> Jesus just **fought with the storm** on the lake, which <u>even fishermen could not control</u>. Jesus is fighting here with a **huge army of evil spirits that** even the <u>whole region cannot control</u>. It was a big fight!

10v) And he begged him earnestly not to send them out of the country. Who won the fight? Jesus! Look at the word "begged." An evil spirit was begging Jesus. <u>That means the evil spirit has already been defeated!</u> Here are ***thousands of evil spirits and a super-tired Jesus***. But **the fight was not competitive!** Many people think Jesus and the evil spirits have equal power! No! **<u>Jesus is superior to any other spirit!</u>** Any other things? **Even nature obeys, and the evil spirits subdue Jesus**! <u>Evil power is stronger than human power, but Jesus is stronger than evil power.</u> **That supreme power is the nature of God. But not just the power; God is love. The supreme love is the nature of God.**

Jesus is loving. (11-13v) "Now a great herd of pigs was feeding there on the hillside, <u>12</u>and they begged him, saying, "Send us to the pigs; let us enter them." <u>13</u>So he gave them permission. And the unclean spirits came out and entered the pigs; and the herd, numbering about two thousand, rushed down the steep bank into the sea and drowned in the sea." Well, do you see love in these verses? Can you guess what kind of place Jesus and the disciples were? Look at what kind of animals there are: **pigs (11v)! This is a gentile land!** Jewish people did not have "pigs." Why? <u>OT law labels pigs as "unclean" animals.</u> They did not eat the pigs, did not sacrifice the pigs either. **It is just "unclean." _So the fact that they have "a large herd of pigs" means that they are not Jewish people_.** The place was, in fact, outside of Jewish Palestine. **They are gentiles**. So here, Jesus is in the gentile place with an "unclean spirit" and an "unclean animal." The worst place he could be. He did not even have a rest. But regardless of the facts and knowing everything, **He came here to save this poor gentile man**!

The demons requested to go to the pigs, and Jesus allowed them, then they went into the pigs and rushed down to the lake. Not just one or two, but **2,000 pigs died!** *Jesus sent* the *"unclean spirit" with the "unclean animal" to save this one man!* More than the thousand lives of the pig, Jesus cared for the life of the "one" gentile man. **Jesus' love for man is more powerful than the evil one!** For the one lost sheep, Jesus would leave the 99 sheep behind to look for the one lost. **To save the "one" soul, Jesus would go anywhere!** Whether it is an "unclean," "uncontrollable," or "**destructive**" place and people, **Jesus would not spare His precious life on the "unclean, uncontrollable, destructive" cross and the tomb! That is the love of God!** That is my love for you!! **Jesus is more powerful than the evil one, but unlike the unloving evil spirit, Jesus is full of love for us! Power and love!** They are the nature of God! Let's look at the last one: the nature of change.

2. **Nature of Change**: (14–15v) The herdsmen fled and told it in the city and in the country. And people came to see what it was that had happened. 15And they came to Jesus and saw the demon-possessed^c man, the one who had had the legion, sitting there, clothed and in his right mind, and they were afraid.

Change is more powerful than the former condition. After all this, the man was changed! Look at how the man was changed. 1) **He was sitting**! That is a miracle! Well, we are all sitting here, but he was not! Day and night, he was wandering off, crying out, and cutting himself. Now, he does not have to do that anymore. He is quietly sitting for the first time in his life! And 2) **he is dressed!** That is a miracle! We are all dressed up here, but he was not. He was naked and undignified. But he is dressed. ***Being dressed means having an identity.*** He belongs to a community. He did not even have his name. His name used to be "Legion, the army of evil spirits," and no one wanted to hang out. But **he has a new identity now**. We still don't know his name, but at least he is dressed. **New...changed identity with dignity, experiencing the power of Jesus!**

When Jesus saves us, **He gives us a new identity with dignity as the children of God**. We used to be slaves to evil spirits, controlled by them. But because of Jesus, we are **clothed with His righteousness**. We **belong to His community, the church, and the Kingdom of God**! But the people were not so excited about this change. Instead of rejoicing, the man became changed; they were afraid. (16-17v) And those who had seen it described to them what had happened to the demon-possessed man and to the pigs. **17**And they began to beg Jesus<u>ᵈ</u> to depart from their region. Just like the **evil spirits**, they _did not want to have any relationship with Jesus_. "**Just leave us alone!**" They are still evil! **They cared more about their business loss—pigs—than** the man. **No love!** They are still evil!

Change promotes love for Jesus. (18v) As he was getting into the boat, the man who had been possessed with demons begged him that he might be with him. But the man was trying to follow Jesus! **He used to beg, "Jesus, leave me alone. Don't torture me." But here, he is begging to follow anywhere he goes**. He did not love Jesus, but **now he loves Jesus**! 19-20v) Jesus did not let him, but said, "And he did not permit him but said to him, "Go home to your friends and tell them how much the Lord has done for you, and how he has had mercy on you." **20**And he went away and began to proclaim in the Decapolis how much Jesus had done for him, and everyone marveled. **Interestingly, Jesus did not allow it this time.** But He said, "**I am your Lord**! Do not follow me; instead, go back to your people (gentile) and tell them about what I have done for you! What **love and mercy** I have shown to you!" **He used to say, "Don't let me leave here!'** But here he obeyed Jesus and went outside. *He went away and went to Decapolis, the gentile territory (outside of Jewish Palestine), to share what God had done for him!* People were amazed. Even before Paul, **he was the first missionary to Gentiles! Jesus' love for him changed him and made him obey what Jesus said.**

Whatever evil nature you have, uncontrollable, destructible sin you are experiencing in your life now, trust the nature of the Lord, who is more powerful and loving than the nature of evil inside of you! He will change you! He will change your nature! *You will love Him and follow Him wherever He is and sends you.* Come and experience His power and love!